This journal belongs to

....

*A*s one of the best loved songs of all time, "Amazing Grace" continues
to touch the hearts of countless people all over the world.
Its lyrics stand as a timeless reminder that God cares about each of us
and knows all the concerns and desires of our hearts.

Through the words of the song and other quotes and Scriptures,
let this journal inspire you to express your thoughts,
record your prayers, embrace God's unconditional love,
and listen to what He is saying to you.
He is as close as breathing.

May the God of amazing grace encourage your heart always.

Amazing Grace

Journal

Ellie Claire
gift & paper expressions

...inspired by life

Amazing grace!
How sweet the sound
That saved a wretch like me!
I once was lost,
but now am found;
Was blind, but now I see.

JOHN NEWTON

For it is by grace you have been saved, through faith—
and this not from yourselves, it is the gift of God—
not by works, so that no one can boast.

EPHESIANS 2:8–9 NIV

So Amazing

Not that we deserve it, not that we can earn it,
but that we know how precious and valuable a gift it is.
That's what makes grace so amazing!

Grace comes free of charge to people who do not deserve it,
and I am one of those people…. Now I am trying
in my own small way to pipe the tune of grace. I do so because I know,
more surely than I know anything, that any pang of healing or forgiveness
or goodness I have ever felt comes solely from the grace of God.

PHILIP YANCEY

May the grace of the Lord Jesus Christ, and the love of God,
and the fellowship of the Holy Spirit be with you all.

2 CORINTHIANS 13:14 NIV

The most glorious promises of God are generally fulfilled
in such a wondrous manner that He steps forth to save us at a time
when there is the least appearance of it.

KARL HEINRICH VON BOGATZKY

Grace is…a boundless offering of God's self to us, suffering with us,
overflowing with tenderness. Grace is God's passion.

GERALD G. MAY

Infinite Love

An infinite God can give all of Himself to each of His children.
He does not distribute Himself that each may have a part, but to each one
He gives all of Himself as fully as if there were no others....
His love has not changed. It hasn't cooled off, and it needs no increase
because He has already loved us with infinite love and there is no way
that infinitude can be increased.... He is the same
yesterday, today, and forever!

A. W. Tozer

Our ever growing soul and its capacities
can be satisfied only in the infinite God.

Sadhu Sundar Singh

Infinite and yet personal, personal and yet infinite,
God may be trusted because He is the True One.
He is true, He acts truly, and He speaks truly.... God's truthfulness
is therefore foundational for His trustworthiness.

Os Guinness

At the very heart and foundation of all God's dealings with us,
however dark and mysterious they may be, we must dare to believe in
and assert the infinite, unmerited, and unchanging love of God.

L. B. Cowman

May you have the power to understand, as all God's people should,
how wide, how long, how high, and how deep his love is.

EPHESIANS 3:18 NLT

God's Favor

God longs to give favor—that is, spiritual strength and health—
to those who seek Him, and Him alone. He grants spiritual favors
and victories, not because the one who seeks Him is holier
than anyone else, but in order to make His holy beauty and His great
redeeming power known…. For it is through the living witness of others
that we are drawn to God at all. It is because of His creatures,
and His work in them, that we come to praise Him.

TERESA OF AVILA

It is not what we do that matters,
but what a sovereign God chooses to do through us.
God doesn't want our success; He wants us.

CHARLES COLSON

Each one of us is God's special work of art. Through us,
He teaches and inspires, delights and encourages, informs and uplifts
all those who view our lives. God, the master artist, is most concerned about
expressing Himself—His thoughts and His intentions—through what
He paints in our character…. [He] wants to paint a beautiful portrait
of His Son in and through your life. A painting like no other in all of time.

JONI EARECKSON TADA

*G*od had special plans for me and set me apart for his work....
He called me through his grace.

GALATIANS 1:15 NCV

Gifts of Grace

Grace is something you can never get but can only be given.
There's no way to earn it or deserve it or bring it about
anymore than you can deserve the taste of raspberries and cream
or earn good looks.... A good night's sleep is grace
and so are good dreams. Most tears are grace.
The smell of rain is grace. Somebody loving you is grace.

FREDERICK BUECHNER

The beauty of grace—our only permanent deliverance from guilt—
is that it meets us where we are and gives us what we don't deserve.

CHARLES R. SWINDOLL

All those who live with any degree of serenity
live by some assurance of grace.

REINHOLD NIEBUHR

Walk in a manner worthy of the calling with which you have been called...
being diligent to preserve the unity of the Spirit in the bond of peace....
To each one of us grace was given according to the measure of Christ's gift.

EPHESIANS 4:1, 3, 7 NASB

Oh, God, give me grace for this day. Not for a lifetime,
nor for next week, nor for tomorrow, just for this day.

MARJORIE HOLMES

The secret of life is that all we have and are
is a gift of grace to be shared.

LLOYD JOHN OGILVIE

All Is Well

It's usually through our hard times, the unexpected and
not-according-to-plan times, that we experience
God in more intimate ways. We discover an unquenchable longing
to know Him more. It's a passion that isn't concerned that life fall
within certain predictable lines, but a passion that pursues God
and knows He is relentless in His pursuit of each one of us.

WENDY MOORE

A living, loving God can and does make His presence felt,
can and does speak to us in the silence of our hearts,
can and does warm and caress us till we no longer doubt
that He is near, that He is here.

BRENNAN MANNING

In difficulties, I can drink freely of God's power
and experience His touch of refreshment and blessing—
much like an invigorating early spring rain.

ANABEL GILLHAM

Lord, you have been our dwelling place
throughout all generations.
Before the mountains were born
or you brought forth the earth and the world,
from everlasting to everlasting you are God.

PSALM 90:1–2 NIV

Before me, even as behind, God is, and all is well.

JOHN GREENLEAF WHITTIER

Give all your worries and cares to God, for he cares about you.

1 PETER 5:7 NLT

Grace and Gratitude

Grace and gratitude belong together like heaven and earth.
Grace evokes gratitude like the voice an echo.
Gratitude follows grace as thunder follows lightning.

KARL BARTH

Life itself, every bit of health that we enjoy, every hour of liberty
and free enjoyment, the ability to see, to hear, to speak, to think,
and to imagine—all this comes from the hand of God.
We show our gratitude by giving back to Him
a part of that which He has given to us.

BILLY GRAHAM

May you be filled with joy, always thanking the Father.
He has enabled you to share in the inheritance
that belongs to his people, who live in the light.

COLOSSIANS 1:11–12 NLT

Gratitude consists in a watchful, minute attention
to the particulars of our state, and to the multitude of God's gifts,
taken one by one. It fills us with a consciousness that God loves
and cares for us, even to the least event and smallest need of life.

HENRY EDWARD MANNING

I will bless the LORD at all times;
His praise shall continually be in my mouth.

PSALM 34:1 NASB

New Way of Life

I pray that the eyes of your heart may be enlightened,
so that you will know what is the hope of His calling,
what are the riches of the glory of His inheritance in the saints,
and what is the surpassing greatness of His power toward us who believe.
These are in accordance with the working of the strength of His might
which He brought about in Christ, when He raised Him from the dead
and seated Him at His right hand in the heavenly places,
far above all rule and authority and power and dominion,
and every name that is named, not only in this age
but also in the one to come.

EPHESIANS 1:18–21 NASB

Since our friendship with God was restored
by the death of his Son while we were still his enemies,
we will certainly be saved through the life of his Son.

ROMANS 5:10 NLT

Just as Christ was raised from the dead
through the glory of the Father, we too may live a new life.

ROMANS 6:4 NIV

$\mathcal{T}$he abundant life that Jesus talked about begins with the unfathomable
Good News put simply: My dear child, I love you anyway.

ALICE CHAPIN

Seek the Lord

If you are seeking after God, you may be sure of this:
God is seeking you much more. He is the Lover, and you are His beloved.
He has promised Himself to you.

JOHN OF THE CROSS

Ask and it will be given to you; seek and you will find;
knock and the door will be opened to you. For everyone who asks receives;
he who seeks finds; and to him who knocks, the door will be opened.

MATTHEW 7:7–8 NIV

Prayer enlarges the heart until it is capable of containing God's
gift of Himself. Ask and seek, and your heart will grow big enough
to receive Him and keep Him as your own.

MOTHER TERESA

Seek the LORD your God, and you will find Him
if you seek Him with all your heart and with all your soul.

DEUTERONOMY 4:29 NKJV

God is not an elusive dream or a phantom to chase,
but a divine person to know. He does not avoid us, but seeks us.
When we seek Him, the contact is instantaneous.

NEVA COYLE

To seek God means first of all to let yourself be found by Him.

I love those who love me; and those
who diligently seek me will find me.

Rich Grace

The LORD gives righteousness and justice
to all who are treated unfairly....
He will not constantly accuse us, nor remain angry forever.
He does not punish us for all our sins;
he does not deal harshly with us, as we deserve.
For his unfailing love toward those who fear him is as great as the height
of the heavens above the earth. He has removed our sins
as far from us as the east is from the west.

PSALM 103:6, 9–12 NLT

By Jesus' gracious, kindly Spirit, He moves in our lives
sharing His very own life with us.... He introduces the exotic fruits
of His own person into the prepared soil of our hearts,
there they take root and flourish.

W. PHILIP KELLER

From the fullness of his grace
we have all received one blessing after another.

JOHN 1:16 NIV

A beautiful life, a rich life, a "worthy" life is, with God's help,
in reach of every man and every woman.

C. WILLIAM FISHER

His overflowing love delights to make us partakers
of the bounties He graciously imparts.

HANNAH MORE

O LORD, be gracious to us; we long for you.
Be our strength every morning.

ISAIAH 33:2 NIV

His Perfection

We don't have to be perfect.... We are asked only to be real,
trusting in His perfection to cover our imperfection,
knowing that one day we will finally be all that Christ
saved us for and wants us to be.

GIGI GRAHAM TCHIVIDJIAN

When perfection comes, the imperfect disappears.... Now we see
but a poor reflection as in a mirror; then we shall see face to face.
Now I know in part; then I shall know fully, even as I am fully known.

1 CORINTHIANS 13:10, 12 NIV

There is no one so far lost that
Jesus cannot find him and cannot save him.

ANDREW MURRAY

God is looking for people who will come in simple dependence
upon His grace, and rest in simple faith upon His greatness.
At this very moment, He's looking at you.

JACK HAYFORD

I am not what I ought to be, I am not what I wish to be,
I am not what I hope to be; but, by the grace of God,
I am not what I was.

JOHN NEWTON

For You have worked wonders, plans formed long ago,
with perfect faithfulness.

ISAIAH 25:1 NASB

God Is Good

All we are and all we have is by the...love of God!
The goodness of God is infinitely more wonderful than
we will ever be able to comprehend.

A. W. Tozer

Open your mouth and taste,
open your eyes and see—how good GOD is.
Blessed are you who run to him. Worship GOD if you want the best;
worship opens doors to all his goodness.

Psalm 34:8–9 MSG

The Lord's goodness surrounds us at every moment.
I walk through it almost with difficulty,
as through thick grass and flowers.

R. W. Barber

All that is good, all that is true, all that is beautiful...be it great or small,
be it perfect or fragmentary, natural as well as supernatural,
moral as well as material, comes from God.

John Henry Newman

We walk without fear, full of hope and courage
and strength to do His will, waiting for the endless good
which He is always giving as fast
as He can get us able to take it in.

George MacDonald

I am still confident of this: I will see
the goodness of the LORD in the land of the living.

PSALM 27:13 NIV

Grace Shines Through

Grace comes into the soul, as the morning sun into the world;
first a dawning, then a light, and at last the sun
in his full and excellent brightness.

THOMAS ADAMS

The growth of grace is like the polishing of metals.
There is first an opaque surface; by and by you see a spark darting out,
then a strong light; till at length it sends back a perfect image
of the sun that shines upon it.

EDWARD PAYSON

Aware of our inbuilt resistance to grace, Jesus talked about it often.
He described a world suffused with God's grace:
where the sun shines on people good and bad;
where birds gather seed gratis,
neither plowing nor harvesting to earn them;
where untended wildflowers burst into bloom on the rocky hillsides.

PHILIP YANCEY

One taper lights a thousand,
Yet shines as it has shone;
And the humblest light may kindle
One brighter than its own.

HEZEKIAH BUTTERWORTH

A pure spirit is a sparkling stream, full of clear thought,
and continually renewed in the crystal river of God's love.

JANET L. SMITH

May God give you more and more grace and peace as you grow in your
knowledge of God and Jesus our Lord.

2 PETER 1:2 NLT

'Twas grace that taught my heart to fear,
And grace my fears relieved;
How precious did that grace appear,
The hour I first believed!

JOHN NEWTON

For the grace of God has appeared, bringing salvation
for all people, training us to renounce ungodliness
and worldly passions, and to live self-controlled,
upright, and godly lives in the present age.

TITUS 2:11-ESV

My Fears Relieved

We sometimes fear to bring our troubles to God,
because they must seem so small to Him who sits
on the circle of the earth. But if they are large enough to…
endanger our welfare, they are large enough
to touch His heart of love.

R. A. TORREY

Grasp the fact that God is for you—let this certainty
make its impact on you in relation to what you are up against
at this very moment; and you will find in thus knowing God
as your sovereign protector, irrevocably committed to you
in the covenant of grace, both freedom from fear
and new strength for the fight.

J. I. PACKER

Faith is simultaneously long perseverance
and unwavering confidence.

PIERRE–YVES EMERY

You can be sure that God will take care of everything you need,
his generosity exceeding even yours in the glory that pours from Jesus.
Our God and Father abounds in glory that just pours out into eternity.

PHILIPPIANS 4:19-20 MSG

Every action of our lives
touches a chord that vibrates in Eternity.

EDWIN HUBBEL CHAPIN

··

··

··

··

··

··

··

··

··

··

··

··

··

··

··

··

··

··

··

Cast your burden on the LORD,
and He shall sustain you.

PSALM 55:22 NKJV

Grace Abounds

The wonder of our Lord is that He is so accessible to us
in the common things of our lives: the cup of water…
breaking of the bread…welcoming children into our arms…
fellowship over a meal…giving thanks. A simple attitude of caring,
listening, and lovingly telling the truth.

NANCIE CARMICHAEL

To pray is to change. This is a great grace. How good of God
to provide a path whereby our lives can be taken over by love
and joy and peace and patience and kindness and goodness
and faithfulness and gentleness and self-control.

RICHARD J. FOSTER

If we believe in Jesus, it is not what we gain,
but what He pours through us that counts.

OSWALD CHAMBERS

For God is, indeed, a wonderful Father who longs
to pour out His mercy upon us, and whose majesty is so great
that He can transform us from deep within.

TERESA OF AVILA

If God is here for us and not elsewhere, then in fact
this place is holy and this moment is sacred.

ISABEL ANDERS

$\mathcal{G}$od is able to make all grace abound to you, so that in all things
at all times…you will abound in every good work.

2 CORINTHIANS 9:8 NIV

Our Father

Incredible as it may seem, God wants our companionship.
He wants to have us close to Him. He wants to be a father to us,
to shield us, to protect us, to counsel us,
and to guide us in our way through life.

BILLY GRAHAM

Don't we all long for a father…
who cares for us in spite of our failures?
We do have that type of a father. A father who is at His best
when we are at our worst…whose grace is strongest
when our devotion is weakest.

MAX LUCADO

This is your Father you are dealing with,
and he knows better than you what you need.
With a God like this loving you, you can pray very simply.

MATTHEW 6:7 MSG

Christ knew His Father and offered Himself
unreservedly into His hands.
If we let ourselves be lost for His sake,
trusting the same God as Lord of all, we shall find safety
where Christ found His, in the arms of the Father.

ELISABETH ELLIOT

....

....

....

....

....

....

....

....

....

....

....

....

....

....

....

....

....

....

....

....

....

Because we are his children, God has sent the Spirit…into our hearts,
prompting us to call out, "Abba, Father."

GALATIANS 4:6 NLT

Blessing on Blessing

God is a rich and bountiful Father,
and He does not forget His children, nor withhold from them
anything which it would be to their advantage to receive.

J. K. MACLEAN

Strength, rest, guidance, grace, help, sympathy, love—
all from God to us! What a list of blessings!

EVELYN STENBOCK

You're blessed when you're content with just who you are—
no more, no less. That's the moment you find yourselves
proud owners of everything that can't be bought.

MATTHEW 5:5 MSG

If anyone would tell you the shortest, surest way
to happiness and all perfection, he must tell you
to make it a rule to yourself to thank and praise God
for everything that happens to you. For it is certain that whatever...
happens to you, if you thank and praise God for it,
you turn it into a blessing.

WILLIAM LAW

God, who is love—who is, if I may say it this way, made out of love—
simply cannot help but shed blessing on blessing upon us.

HANNAH WHITALL SMITH

I will send down showers in season;
there will be showers of blessing.

EZEKIEL 34:26 NIV

Through His Creation

It is an extraordinary and beautiful thing that God, in creation...
works with the beauty of matter; the reality of things;
the discoveries of the senses, all five of them;
so that we, in turn, may hear the grass growing;
see a face springing to life in love and laughter....
The offerings of creation...our glimpses of truth.

MADELEINE L'ENGLE

I am convinced that God has built into all of us
an appreciation of beauty and has even allowed us
to participate in the creation of beautiful things and places.
It may be one way God brings healing to our brokenness,
and a way that we can contribute toward
bringing wholeness to our fallen world.

MARY JANE WORDEN

I have known art and beauty, music and gladness;
I have known friendship and love and family ties;
but it is certain that till we see God in the world—
God in the bright and boundless universe—
we never know the highest joy.

ORVILLE DEWEY

Seeing how God works in nature
can help us understand how He works in our lives.

JANETTE OKE

*Honor and majesty surround him;
strength and beauty fill his sanctuary.*

PSALM 96:6 NLT

Blessed Assurance

Peace of conscience, liberty of heart, the sweetness
of abandoning ourselves in the hands of God,
the joy of always seeing the light grow in our hearts,
finally, freedom from the fears and insatiable desires of the times,
multiply a hundredfold the happiness which
the true children of God possess in the midst of their [trials],
if they are faithful.

FRANÇOIS FÉNELON

God Incarnate is the end of fear;
and the heart that realizes that He is in the midst,
that takes heed to the assurance of His loving presence,
will be quiet in the midst of alarm.

F. B. MEYER

This is the secret: Christ lives in you.
This gives you assurance of sharing his glory.

COLOSSIANS 1:27 NLT

Come, Thou long-expected Jesus,
born to set Thy people free;
From our fears and sins release us;
let us find our rest in Thee.

CHARLES WESLEY

Today I give it all to Jesus: my precious children, my mate, my hopes,
my plans and dreams and schemes, my fears and failures—all.
Peace and contentment come when the struggle ceases.

GLORIA GAITHER

In peace I will lie down and sleep,
for you alone, O Lᴏʀᴅ, will keep me safe.

Pꜱᴀʟᴍ 4:8 ɴʟᴛ

Trust Always

There is an activity of the spirit, silent, unseen,
which must be the dynamic of any form of truly creative, fruitful trust.
When we commit a predicament, a possibility, a person to God
in genuine confidence, we do not merely step aside and tap our foot
until God comes through. We remain involved.
We remain in contact with God in gratitude and praise.

EUGENIA PRICE

I trust You always though I may seem to be lost and in the shadow of death.
I will not fear, for You are ever with me. And You will never leave me
to face my perils alone.

THOMAS MERTON

Yea, though I walk through the valley of the shadow of death,
I will fear no evil; for You are with me;
Your rod and Your staff, they comfort me.

PSALM 23:4 NKJV

Trust in your Redeemer's strength…exercise what faith you have,
and by and by He shall rise upon you with healing beneath His wings.
Go from faith to faith and you shall receive blessing upon blessing.

CHARLES H. SPURGEON

*T*rust in the LORD with all your heart;
and lean not on your own understanding.

PROVERBS 3:5 NKJV

Encountering God

We encounter God in the ordinariness of life, not in the search
for spiritual highs and extraordinary, mystical experiences,
but in our simple presence in life.

BRENNAN MANNING

Much of what is sacred is hidden in the ordinary,
everyday moments of our lives. To see something of the sacred
in those moments takes slowing down
so we can live our lives more reflectively.

KEN GIRE

It is through man's encounter with God
that he reaches his highest destiny.

CAROL GISH

God is with us in the midst of our daily, routine lives.
In the middle of cleaning the house or driving somewhere in the pickup....
Often it's in the middle of the most mundane task
that He lets us know He is there with us. We realize, then,
that there can be no "ordinary" moments
for people who live their lives with Jesus.

MICHAEL CARD

If each moment is sacred—
a time and place where we encounter God—
life itself is sacred.

JEAN M. BLOMQUIST

This is how we experience his deep
and abiding presence in us: by the Spirit he gave us.

1 JOHN 3:24 MSG

His Loving Touch

The simple fact of being…in the presence of the Lord
and of showing Him all that I think, feel, sense, and experience,
without trying to hide anything, must please Him.
Somehow, somewhere, I know that He loves me, even though
I do not feel that love as I can feel a human embrace, even though
I do not hear a voice as I hear human words of consolation.…
God is greater than my senses, greater than my thoughts,
greater than my heart. I do believe that He touches me in places
that are unknown even to myself.

HENRI J. M. NOUWEN

God's fingers can touch nothing but to mold it into loveliness.

GEORGE MACDONALD

God is here! I hear His voice
While thrushes make the woods rejoice.
I touch His robe each time I place
My hand against a pansy's face.
I breathe His breath if I but pass
Verbenas trailing through the grass.
God is here! From every tree
His leafy fingers beckon me.

MADELEINE AARON

It is not objective proof of God's existence that we want
but the experience of God's presence.
That is the miracle we are really after, and that is also,
I think, the miracle that we really get.

FREDERICK BUECHNER

God's Spirit touches our spirits and confirms who we really are.
We know who he is, and we know who we are: Father and children.

ROMANS 8:16 MSG

God of Promise

For as the rain comes down,
and the snow from heaven,
and do not return there,
but water the earth,
and make it bring forth and bud,
that it may give seed to the sower
and bread to the eater,
so shall My word be
that goes forth from My mouth;
it shall not return to Me void,
but it shall accomplish what I please,
and it shall prosper in the thing
for which I sent it.

ISAIAH 55:10–11 NKJV

God writes with a pen that never blots,
speaks with a tongue that never slips,
and acts with a hand that never fails.

HUBERT VAN ZELLER

Be assured, if you walk with Him and look to Him
and expect help from Him, He will never fail you.

GEORGE MUELLER

God is the God of promise. He keeps His word,
even when that seems impossible.

COLIN URQUHART

The Lord always keeps his promises;
he is gracious in all he does.

Psalm 145:13 nlt

Countless Beauties

Be still, and in the quiet moments, listen to the voice
of your heavenly Father. His words can renew your spirit....
No one knows you and your needs like He does.

JANET L. SMITH

Lord...give me the gift of faith
to be renewed and shared with others each day.
Teach me to live this moment only,
looking neither to the past with regret,
nor the future with apprehension.
Let love be my aim and my life a prayer.

ROSEANN ALEXANDER-ISHAM

One thing I ask of the LORD, this is what I seek:
that I may dwell in the house of the LORD all the days of my life,
to gaze upon the beauty of the LORD.

PSALM 27:4 NIV

Our Creator would never have made such lovely days,
and given us the deep hearts to enjoy them,
above and beyond all thought,
unless we were meant to be immortal.

NATHANIEL HAWTHORNE

The joyful birds prolong the strain,
their song with every spring renewed;
the air we breathe, and falling rain,
each softly whispers: God is good.

JOHN HAMPDEN GURNEY

Worship the LORD in the beauty of holiness!

PSALM 96:9 NKJV

All the world is an utterance of the Almighty. Its countless beauties, its exquisite adaptations, all speak to you of Him.

PHILLIPS BROOKS

Dare to Believe

Regardless of whether we feel strong or weak in our faith,
we remember that our assurance is not based
upon our ability to conjure up some special feeling.
Rather, it is built upon a confident assurance in the faithfulness of God.
We focus on His trustworthiness and especially on His steadfast love.

RICHARD J. FOSTER

So faith bounds forward to its goal in God,
and love can trust her Lord to lead her there;
upheld by Him my soul is following hard,
till God has fully fulfilled my deepest prayer.

FREDERICK BROOK

The grace is God's: the faith is ours.
God gave us the free will with which to choose.
God gave us the capacity to believe and trust.

BILLY GRAHAM

Faith isn't the ability to believe long and far into the misty future.
It's simply taking God at His word and taking the next step.

JONI EARECKSON TADA

There is no unbelief.
Whoever plants a seed beneath the sod,
And waits to see it push away the clod,
He trusts in God.

ELIZABETH YORK CASE

Faith is not belief without proof,
but trust without reservations.

ELTON TRUEBLOOD

....

....

....

....

....

....

....

....

....

....

....

....

....

....

....

....

....

....

I trust in your unfailing love.
I will rejoice because you have rescued me.

PSALM 13:5 NLT

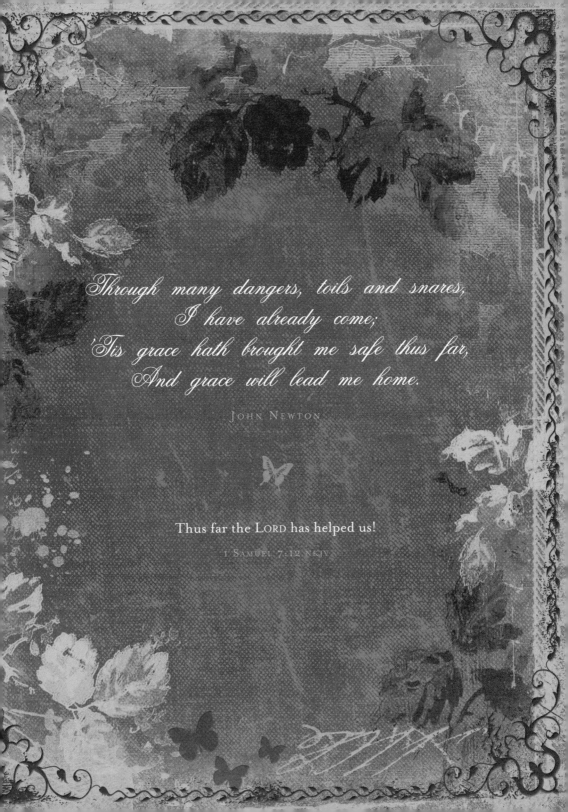

Through many dangers, toils and snares,
I have already come;
'Tis grace hath brought me safe thus far,
And grace will lead me home.

John Newton

Thus far the LORD has helped us!

1 Samuel 7:12 NKJV

God's Nearness

Do you believe that God is near? He wants you to.
He wants you to know that He is in the midst of your world.
Wherever you are as you read these words, He is present. In your car.
On the plane. In your office, your bedroom,
your den. He's near. And He is more than near. He is active.

MAX LUCADO

I have sought Thy nearness;
With all my heart have I called Thee,
And going out to meet Thee
I found Thee coming toward me.

YEHUDA HALEVI

We need never shout across the spaces to an absent God.
He is nearer than our own soul,
closer than our most secret thoughts.

A. W. TOZER

Have confidence in God's mercy, for when you think
He is a long way from you, He is often quite near.

THOMAS À KEMPIS

God still draws near to us in the ordinary, commonplace,
everyday experiences and places.... He comes in surprising ways.

HENRY GARIEPY

It is God to whom and with whom we travel, and while He
is the End of our journey, He is also at every stopping place.

ELISABETH ELLIOT

*D*raw near to God and He will draw near to you.

JAMES 4:8 NASB

Redeemed

Praise the LORD, O my soul,
and forget not all his benefits—
who forgives all your sins
and heals all your diseases,
who redeems your life from the pit
and crowns you with love and compassion,
who satisfies your desires with good things
so that your youth is renewed like the eagle's.

PSALM 103:2–5 NIV

I think of my blessed Redeemer,
I think of Him all the day long:
I sing, for I cannot be silent;
His love is the theme of my song.

FANNY CROSBY

When we focus on God, the scene changes.
He's in control of our lives; nothing lies outside
the realm of His redemptive grace. Even when we make mistakes,
fail in relationships, or deliberately make bad choices,
God can redeem us.

PENELOPE J. STOKES

Jesus is the Savior, but He is even more than that!
He is more than a Forgiver of our sins.
He is even more than our Provider of eternal life.
He is our Redeemer! He is the One who is ready to recover
and restore what the power of sin and death has taken from us.

JACK HAYFORD

The Lord will redeem those who serve him.
No one who takes refuge in him will be condemned.

PSALM 34:22 NLT

Grace Is Power

Grace is the central invitation to life and the final word.
It's the beckoning nudge and the overwhelming,
undeserved mercy that urges us to change and grow,
and then gives us the power to pull it off.

TIM HANSEL

Grace is not simply leniency when we have sinned.
Grace is the enabling gift of God not to sin.
Grace is power, not just pardon.

JOHN PIPER

Grace is an energy; not a mere sentiment; not a mere
thought of the Almighty; not even a word of the Almighty.
It is as real an energy as the energy of electricity.
It is a divine energy; it is the energy of the divine affection
rolling in plenteousness toward the shores of human need.

BENJAMIN JOWETT

Look for, long for, pray for, and expect
special breaking-through times when
God makes His presence very real, very powerful!
And until they come, dwell in His presence by faith
and gaze upon His beauty.

RAY AND ANNE ORTLUND

Grace is given not because we have done good works,
but in order that we may be able to do them.

AUGUSTINE

*B*y God's grace and mighty power, I have been given the privilege
of serving him by spreading this Good News.

EPHESIANS 3:7 NLT

He Leads Me

Living a life of faith means never knowing where you are being led.
But it does mean loving and knowing the One who is leading. It is literally
a life of faith…a life of knowing Him who calls us to go.

OSWALD CHAMBERS

A new path lies before us;
We're not sure where it leads;
But God goes on before us,
Providing all our needs.
This path, so new, so different
Exciting as we climb,
Will guide us in His perfect will
Until the end of time.

LINDA MAURICE

God guides us, despite our uncertainties and our vagueness,
even through our failings and mistakes…. He leads us step by step,
from event to event. Only afterwards, as we look back
over the way we have come and reconsider
certain important moments in our lives
in the light of all that has followed them,
or when we survey the whole progress of our lives,
do we experience the feeling of having been led without knowing it,
the feeling that God has mysteriously guided us.

PAUL TOURNIER

Lead me by your truth and teach me, for you are
the God who saves me. All day long I put my hope in you.

PSALM 25:5 NLT

Shining Promises

Our feelings do not affect God's facts.
They may blow up, like clouds, and cover the eternal things
that we do most truly believe.
We may not see the shining of the promises—
but they still shine! [His strength] is not for one moment less
because of our human weakness.

AMY CARMICHAEL

We do not know how this is true—where would faith be if we did?—
but we do know that all things that happen are full of shining seed.
Light is sown for us—not darkness.

But He knows the way I take; when He has tried me,
I shall come forth as gold.

JOB 23:10 NASB

God's promises are like the stars;
the darker the night the brighter they shine.

DAVID NICHOLAS

God has not promised skies always blue,
flower-strewn pathways all our lives through;
God has not promised sun without rain,
joy without sorrow, peace without pain.
But God has promised strength for the day,
rest for the labor, light for the way,
grace for the trials, help from above,
unfailing sympathy, undying love.

ANNIE JOHNSON FLINT

Not one word has failed of all His good promise.

1 KINGS 8:56 NASB

Strong Refuge

We know that [God] gives us every grace, every abundant grace;
and though we are so weak of ourselves, this grace is able to carry us
through every obstacle and difficulty.

The LORD is good, a strong refuge when trouble comes.
He is close to those who trust in him.

NAHUM 1:7 NLT

If the Lord be with us, we have no cause of fear. His eye is upon us,
His arm over us, His ear open to our prayer—His grace sufficient,
His promise unchangeable.

JOHN NEWTON

Jesus Christ is no security against storms,
but He is perfect security in storms.
He has never promised you an easy passage,
only a safe landing.

L. B. COWMAN

Do not take over much thought for tomorrow.
God, who has led you safely on so far,
will lead you on to the end. Be altogether at rest
in the loving holy confidence which you ought to have
in His heavenly Providence.

FRANCIS DE SALES

You are my strong refuge. My mouth is filled
with Your praise and with Your glory all day long.

PSALM 71:7–8 NASB

God Is For Us

When you're in over your head,
I'll be there with you.
When you're in rough waters,
you will not go down.
When you're between a rock and a hard place,
it won't be a dead end—
Because I am GOD, your personal God,
The Holy of Israel, your Savior.
I paid a huge price for you…!
That's how much you mean to me!
That's how much I love you!

ISAIAH 43:2–4 MSG

God not only knows us, but He values us highly in spite of all He knows….
You and I are the creatures He prizes above the rest of His creation.
We are made in His image and He sacrificed His Son
that each one of us might be one with Him.

JOHN FISHER

Lord Jesus Christ, I thank You
For all the benefits You have won for me,
For all the pains and insults that
You have borne for me.
Most merciful redeemer, friend and brother,
May I know You more clearly,
Love You more dearly
And follow You more nearly
Day by day. Amen.

RICHARD OF CHICHESTER

If God is for us, who can be against us?

ROMANS 8:31 NKJV

Restoring Love

God's loving initiative to step into time and space
to restore us to Himself is still a cause for wonder and praise.

GLORIA GAITHER

There is no rest in the heart of God
until He knows that we are at rest in His grace.

LLOYD JOHN OGILVIE

Keep a firm grip on the faith. The suffering won't last forever.
It won't be long before this generous God who has great plans for us
in Christ—eternal and glorious plans they are!—will have you
put together and on your feet for good.

1 PETER 5:10–11 MSG

Guidance is a sovereign act. Not merely does
God will to guide us by showing us His way…
whatever mistakes we may make, we shall come safely home.
Slippings and strayings there will be, no doubt,
but the everlasting arms are beneath us;
we shall be caught, rescued, restored. This is God's promise;
this is how good He is. And our self-distrust,
while keeping us humble, must not cloud
the joy with which we lean on our faithful covenant God.

J. I. PACKER

The LORD longs to be gracious to you;
he rises to show you compassion.

ISAIAH 30:18 NIV

Every Need

God wants nothing from us except our needs,
and these furnish Him with room to display His bounty
when He supplies them freely.... Not what I have,
but what I do not have, is the first point of contact
between my soul and God.

CHARLES H. SPURGEON

Jesus Christ has brought every need, every joy,
every gratitude, every hope of ours before God.
He accompanies us and brings us into the presence of God.

DIETRICH BONHOEFFER

You can trust God right now to supply all your needs for today.
And if your needs are more tomorrow, His supply will be greater also.

Knowing God is putting your trust in Him. Trust that He loves you
and will provide for your every need. When we know God, we know Him
like a personal friend.... God is for us! He will never leave us.

TOM RICHARDS

Each of us may be sure that if God sends us on stony paths
He will provide us with strong shoes, and He will not send us
out on any journey for which He does not equip us well.

ALEXANDER MACLAREN

You are my strength; I wait for you to rescue me,
for you, O God, are my fortress.

PSALM 59:9 NLT

Boundless Grace

We can no more take in a supply of grace for the future
than we can eat enough today to last us for the next six months,
nor can we inhale sufficient air into our lungs with one breath
to sustain life for a week to come. We are permitted
to draw upon God's store of grace from day to day as we need it.

DWIGHT L. MOODY

On the inside, where God is making new life,
not a day goes by without his unfolding grace.

2 CORINTHIANS 4:16 MSG

The grace of God is infinite and eternal.
As it had no beginning, so it can have no end,
and being an attribute of God, it is as boundless as infinitude.

A. W. TOZER

The duties God requires of us are not
in proportion to the strength we possess in ourselves.
Rather, they are proportional to the resources
available to us in Christ. We do not have the ability
in ourselves to accomplish the least of God's tasks.
This is a law of grace. When we recognize it is impossible
to perform a duty in our own strength,
we will discover the secret of its accomplishment.

JOHN OWEN

As God is unlimited in goodness,
He should have our unlimited love.

HANNAH MORE

Surpassing Grace

Grace is no stationary thing, it is ever becoming.
It is flowing straight out of God's heart. Grace does nothing
but re-form and convey God. Grace makes the soul
conformable to the will of God. God, the ground of the soul,
and grace go together.

MEISTER ECKHART

From the word "grace" we can spell out its meaning so clearly:
God's Riches At Christ's Expense. And even better, those riches are not
a far-off paradise we have to wait for but resources that we have right now.
Christ's loving sacrifice empowers us to live today, fully alive.

BARBARA FARMER

Grace means that God already loves us as much as
an infinite God can possibly love.

PHILIP YANCEY

Give us grace, almighty Father, to address You
With all our hearts as well as with our lips.
You are present everywhere:
From You no secrets can be hidden.
Teach us to fix our thoughts on You,
Reverently and with love.

JANE AUSTEN

Grace is a profound gift of life to mankind that brings
the original intent of our existence to fulfillment—
to bear the image of God on the earth,
and thereby to fill the earth with God's glory.

DEBORAH WEBB

The LORD is compassionate and gracious,
slow to anger, abounding in love.

PSALM 103:8 NIV

Safe Shelter

After a hard day scrambling to find your way around the world,
it's assuring to come home to a place you know.
God can be equally familiar to you. With time you can learn
where to go for nourishment, where to hide for protection,
where to turn for guidance. Just as your earthly house
is a place of refuge, so God's house is a place of peace.

MAX LUCADO

Why would God promise a refuge unless He knew
we would need a place to hide once in a while?

NEVA COYLE

Hidden in the hollow of His blessed hand,
Never foe can follow, never traitor stand;
Not a surge of worry, not a shade of care,
Not a blast of hurry touch the spirit there.

FRANCES RIDLEY HAVERGAL

I know that He who is far outside the whole creation
Takes me within Himself and hides me in His arms....
He is my heart, He is in heaven: Both there and here
He shows Himself to me with equal glory.

SYMEON

....

....

....

....

....

....

....

....

....

....

....

....

....

....

....

....

....

....

....

....

....

*K*eep me as the apple of Your eye;
hide me under the shadow of Your wings.

PSALM 17:8 NKJV

The Lord has promised good to me.
His word my hope secures;
He will my shield and portion be,
As long as life endures.

John Newton

God's way is perfect. All the LORD's promises prove true.
He is a shield for all who look to him for protection.

2 Samuel 22:31 NLT

Unshakable Promises

Commit to hope. There's reason to! For the believer,
hope is divinely assured things that aren't here yet!
Our hope is grounded in unshakable promises.

JACK HAYFORD

Faith allows us to continually delight in life
since we have placed our needs in God's hands.

JANET L. SMITH

Confidence is not based on wishful thinking,
but in knowing that God is in control.

Remember you are very special to God as His precious child.
He has promised to complete the good work He has begun in you.
As you continue to grow in Him, He will teach you
to be a blessing to others.

GARY SMALLEY AND JOHN TRENT

God promises to keep us in the palm of [His] hand,
with or without our awareness. God has already made a space for us,
even if we have not made a space for God.

DAVID AND BARBARA SORENSEN

There are no hidden reserves in the promises of God
that are meant to deprive them of their complete fulfillment.

HANNAH WHITALL SMITH

*L*et us hold tightly without wavering to the hope we affirm,
for God can be trusted to keep his promise.

HEBREWS 10:23 NLT

Personal Grace

All that we have and are is one of the unique
and never-to-be repeated ways God has chosen
to express Himself in space and time. Each of us,
made in His image and likeness, is yet another promise
He has made to the universe that He will continue
to love it and care for it.

BRENNAN MANNING

You have a unique message to deliver, a unique song to sing,
a unique act of love to bestow. This message, this song, and this act of love
have been entrusted exclusively to the one and only you.

JOHN POWELL

We have missed the full impact of the Gospel
if we have not discovered what it is to be ourselves,
loved by God, irreplaceable in His sight,
unique among our fellow men.

BRUCE LARSON

Priceless in value, we are handcrafted by God,
who has a personal design and plan for each of us.

WENDY MOORE

Everyone has a unique role to fill in the world
and is important in some respect.
Everyone, including and perhaps especially you, is indispensable.

NATHANIEL HAWTHORNE

For we are God's workmanship,
created in Christ Jesus to do good works.

EPHESIANS 2:10 NIV

Grace Is Enough

Lord…You have given me anything I am or have;
I give it all back to You to stand under Your will alone.
Your love and Your grace are enough for me;
I shall ask for nothing more.

IGNATIUS OF LOYOLA

My grace is sufficient for you,
for My strength is made perfect in weakness.

2 CORINTHIANS 12:9 NKJV

Let your faith in Christ…be in the quiet confidence
that He will every day and every moment keep you as the apple of His eye,
keep you in perfect peace and in the sure experience of all the light
and the strength you need in His service.

ANDREW MURRAY

The Creator thinks enough of you
to have sent Someone very special so that you might have life—
abundantly, joyfully, completely, and victoriously.

I have come that they may have life,
and that they may have it more abundantly.

JOHN 10:10 NKJV

Some days, it is enough encouragement just to watch the clouds
break up and disappear, leaving behind a blue patch of sky
and bright sunshine that is so warm upon my face.
It's a glimpse of divinity; a kiss from heaven.

Let the beloved of the LORD rest secure in him,
for he shields him all day long.

DEUTERONOMY 33:12 NIV

God Is Patient

God is waiting for us to come to Him with our needs....
God's throne room is always open....
Every single believer in the whole world
could walk into the throne room all at one time,
and it would not even be crowded.

CHARLES STANLEY

Lift up your eyes. Your heavenly Father waits to bless you—
in inconceivable ways to make your life
what you never dreamed it could be.

ANNE ORTLUND

God has put into each of our lives a void that cannot be filled by the world.
We may leave God or put Him on hold, but He is always there,
patiently waiting for us...to turn back to Him.

EMILIE BARNES

To the Lord one day is as a thousand years,
and a thousand years is as one day. The Lord is not slow
in doing what he promised—the way some people understand slowness.
But God is being patient with you. He does not want anyone to be lost,
but he wants all people to change their hearts and lives.

2 PETER 3:8–9 NCV

God waits for us in the inner sanctuary of the soul.
He welcomes us there.

RICHARD J. FOSTER

God is kind and merciful...
this most patient God, extravagant in love.

JOEL 2:13 MSG

My Father's World

When I look at the galaxies on a clear night—when I look
at the incredible brilliance of creation, and think that this is what God is like,
then instead of feeling intimidated and diminished by it, I am enlarged—
I rejoice that I am part of it.

MADELEINE L'ENGLE

This is my Father's world;
He shines in all that's fair.
In the rustling grass I hear Him pass;
He speaks to me everywhere.

MALTBIE D. BABCOCK

Nothing can give you quite the same thrill
as the feeling that you are in harmony
with the great God of the universe who created all things.

DR. JAMES DOBSON

How beautiful it is to be alive!
To wake each morn as if the Maker's grace
Did us afresh from nothingness derive.
That we might sing "How happy is our case!
How beautiful it is to be alive."

HENRY SEPTIMUS SUTTON

Above all give me grace to use these beauties of earth without me
and this eager stirring of life within me as a means whereby my soul may rise
from creature to Creator, and from nature to nature's God.

JOHN BAILLIE

The earth is the LORD's, and all its fullness,
The world and those who dwell therein.

PSALM 24:1 NKJV

Wherever You Go

He is the God who made the world and everything in it....
From one man he created all the nations throughout the whole earth....
His purpose was for the nations to seek after God
and perhaps feel their way toward him and find him—
though he is not far from any one of us.

ACTS 17:24, 26–27 NLT

Something deep in all of us yearns for God's beauty,
and we can find it no matter where we are.

SUE MONK KIDD

Wherever we look in the realm of nature,
we see evidence for God's design
and exquisite care for His creatures.
Whether we examine the cosmos on its largest scale
or its tiniest, His handiwork is evident....
God's fingerprints are visible.

DR. HUGH ROSS

I feel simply carried along each hour, doing my part in a plan
which is far beyond myself. This sense of cooperation with God
in little things is what so astonishes me, for I never have felt this way before.
I need something, and turn around to find it waiting for me.
I must work, to be sure, but there is God working along with me.

FRANK LAUBACH

I am with you and will watch over you wherever you go.

GENESIS 28:15 NIV

River of Delights

Your love, O LORD, reaches to the heavens,
your faithfulness to the skies.
Your righteousness is like the mighty mountains,
your justice like the great deep....
How priceless is your unfailing love!
Both high and low among men
find refuge in the shadow of your wings.
They feast on the abundance of your house;
you give them drink from your river of delights.
For with you is the fountain of life;
in your light we see light.

PSALM 36:5–9 NIV

God loves us, not because we are lovable but because He is love,
not because He needs to receive but because He delights to give.

C. S. LEWIS

From God, great and small, rich and poor, draw living water
from a living spring, and those who serve Him freely and gladly
will receive grace answering to grace.

THOMAS À KEMPIS

God's love is like a river springing up in the Divine Substance
and flowing endlessly through His creation, filling all things
with life and goodness and strength.

THOMAS MERTON

$\mathcal{T}$he water I give will be an artesian spring within,
gushing fountains of endless life.

JOHN 4:14 MSG

Promises Fulfilled

The fulfillment of God's promise depends entirely
on trusting God and his way, and then simply
embracing him and what he does.
God's promise arrives as pure gift.

ROMANS 4:16 MSG

Jesus Christ opens wide the doors of the treasure house of God's promises,
and bids us go in and take with boldness the riches that are ours.

CORRIE TEN BOOM

God has promised us even more than His own Son. He's promised us power
through the Spirit—power that will help us do all that He asks of us.

JONI EARECKSON TADA

We may...depend upon God's promises, for...
He will be as good as His word. He is so kind that He
cannot deceive us, so true that He cannot break His promise.

MATTHEW HENRY

Not one word of all the good words
which the LORD your God spoke concerning you has failed;
all have been fulfilled for you, not one of them has failed.

JOSHUA 23:14 NASB

Tarry at the promise till God meets you there.
He always returns by way of His promises.

L. B. COWMAN

*Y*our promises have been thoroughly tested;
that is why I love them so much.

PSALM 119:140 NLT

A Gift to Cherish

Make the least of all that goes and the most of all that comes.
Don't regret what is past. Cherish what you have. Look forward
to all that is to come. And most important of all,
rely moment by moment on Jesus Christ.

GIGI GRAHAM TCHIVIDJIAN

Everything in life is most fundamentally a gift. And you receive it best,
and you live it best, by holding it with very open hands.

LEO O'DONOVAN

People should eat and drink and enjoy the fruits of their labor,
for these are gifts from God.

ECCLESIASTES 3:13 NLT

Time is a very precious gift of God; so precious
that it's only given to us moment by moment.

AMELIA BARR

Your life is a gift from God,
And it is a privilege to share it.
Today and always,
Know that you have a
Very special place in others' hearts—

And in His.

Live your life while you have it. Life is a splendid gift—
there is nothing small about it.

FLORENCE NIGHTINGALE

The free gift of God is eternal life
through Christ Jesus our Lord.

ROMANS 6:23 NLT

The Source

He is the Source. Of everything. Strength for your day. Wisdom for your task.
Comfort for your soul. Grace for your battle. Provision for each need.
Understanding for each failure. Assistance for every encounter.

JACK HAYFORD

We are forgiven and righteous because of Christ's sacrifice;
therefore we are pleasing to God in spite of our failures.
Christ alone is the source of our forgiveness, freedom, joy, and purpose.

ROBERT S. MCGEE

God is the Beginning—not just the starting point,
but the Source of all things.

MARILYN M. MORGAN

We must drink deeply from the very Source the deep calm
and peace of interior quietude and refreshment of God,
allowing the pure water of divine grace to flow plentifully
and unceasingly from the Source itself.

MOTHER TERESA

You are never alone. In your heart of hearts, in the place
where no two people are ever alike, Christ is waiting for you.
And what you never dared hope for springs to life.

BROTHER ROGER OF TAIZÉ

The very life of God, epitomized in the love of God,
originates only and always with Him.

W. PHILIP KELLER

For he satisfies the thirsty
and fills the hungry with good things.

PSALM 107:9 NLT

Who Am I?

Understanding your identity produces a desire
for intimate fellowship with your heavenly Father.
If you don't know who you are, you may see yourself
as a servant who must make restitution for sin.
Servants find it difficult to enjoy an intimate love relationship
with their masters. However, sons and fathers are
able to enjoy each other. Do you see yourself
primarily as God's child or as His servant?

And while he was still a long way off,
his father saw him coming. Filled with love and compassion,
he ran to his son, embraced him, and kissed him.

LUKE 15:20 NLT

If we are children of God, we have a tremendous treasure in nature
and will realize that it is holy and sacred.
We will see God reaching out to us in every wind that blows,
every sunrise and sunset, every cloud in the sky,
every flower that blooms, and every leaf that fades.

OSWALD CHAMBERS

We think God's love rises and falls with our performance. It doesn't....
He loves you for whose you are: you are His child.

MAX LUCADO

How great is the love the Father has lavished on us, that we should
be called children of God! And that is what we are!

1 JOHN 3:1 NIV

New Light

Into all our lives, in many simple, familiar…ways,
God infuses this element of joy from the surprises of life,
which unexpectedly brighten our days, and fill our eyes with light.

SAMUEL LONGFELLOW

Each time a rainbow appears, stretching
from one end of the sky to the other, it's God renewing His promise.
Each shade of color, each facet of light displays the radiant spectrum
of God's love—a promise that life can be new for each one of us.

Brightness of my Father's glory,
Sunshine of my Father's face,
Let Your glory e'er shine on me,
Fill me with Your grace.

JEAN SOPHIA PIGOTT

It doesn't take a huge spotlight to draw attention to how great our God is.
All it takes is for one committed person to so let His light shine before men,
that a world lost in darkness welcomes the light.

GARY SMALLEY AND JOHN TRENT

The day is done, the sun has set,
Yet light still tints the sky;
My heart stands still
In reverence,
For God is passing by.

RUTH ALLA WAGER

*Every good and perfect gift is from above,
coming down from the Father of the heavenly lights.*

JAMES 1:17 NIV

Yea, when this flesh and heart shall fail,
And mortal life shall cease;
I shall possess, within the vail,
A life of joy and peace.

JOHN NEWTON

So let us come boldly to the throne of our gracious God.
There we will receive his mercy, and we will find grace
to help us when we need it most.

HEBREWS 4:16 NLT

A Living Witness

My love of You, O Lord, is not some vague feeling:
it is positive and certain. Your word struck into my heart
and from that moment I loved You. Besides this, all about me,
heaven and earth and all that they contain proclaim that I should love You.

AUGUSTINE

God's children who joyously know and claim who they are
and whose they are, will be most likely to manifest the family likeness,
just because they know they are His children.

ALICE CHAPIN

We are His only witnesses. God is counting on each of us.
No angel has been given the job. We are the lanterns—
Christ is the light inside.

OLETA SPRAY

It is through the living witness of others that we are drawn to God at all.
It is because of His creatures, and His work in them,
that we come to praise Him.

TERESA OF AVILA

I cannot witness that I have entered fully
into this life of perpetual communion with the Father,
but I have caught enough glimpses that I know it to be the best,
the finest, the fullest way of living.

RICHARD J. FOSTER

*S*ing to the LORD, praise his name;
proclaim his salvation day after day.

PSALM 96:2 NIV

Eternal Love

The LORD is like a father to his children,
tender and compassionate to those who fear him.
For he knows how weak we are;
he remembers we are only dust.
Our days on earth are like grass;
like wildflowers, we bloom and die.
The wind blows, and we are gone—
as though we had never been here.
But the love of the LORD remains forever....
The LORD has made the heavens his throne;
from there he rules over everything.

PSALM 103:13–17, 19 NLT

Amid the ebb and flow of the passing world,
our God remains unmoved, and His throne endures forever.

ROBERT COLEMAN

The reason we can dare to risk loving others is that
"God has for Christ's sake loved us." Think of it!
We are loved eternally, totally, individually, unreservedly!
Nothing can take God's love away.

GLORIA GAITHER

The impetus of God's love comes from within Himself,
to share with us His life and love. It is a beautiful, eternal gift,
held out to us in the hands of love. All we have to do is say "Yes!"

JOHN POWELL

*H*e loves us with unfailing love;
the LORD's faithfulness endures forever.

PSALM 117:2 NLT

Grace Extended

In whatever [God] does in the course of our lives, He gives us,
through the experience, some power to help others.

ELISABETH ELLIOT

It helps, now and then, to step back and take a long view.
The kingdom [of God] is not only beyond our efforts,
it is even beyond our vision. We accomplish in our lifetime
only a tiny fraction of the magnificent enterprise that is God's work.
Nothing we do is complete, which is a way of saying that the kingdom
always lies beyond us…. We cannot do everything, and there is
a sense of liberation in realizing that. This enables us to do something,
and to do it very well. It may be incomplete,
but it is a beginning, a step along the way, an opportunity
for the Lord's grace to enter and do the rest.
We may never see the end results, but that is the difference
between the master builder and the worker. We are workers,
not master builders; ministers, not messiahs.
We are prophets of a future not our own.

OSCAR ROMERO

Faith in God gives your life a center from which
you can reach out and dare to love the world.

BARBARA FARMER

If I can stop one Heart from breaking
I shall not live in vain
If I can ease one Life the Aching
or cool one Pain
Or help one fainting Robin
Unto his Nest again
I shall not live in Vain.

EMILY DICKINSON

Strength is for service, not status. Each one of us needs to look after the good of the people around us, asking ourselves, "How can I help?"

ROMANS 15:1–2 MSG

Joy and Peace

God came to us because God wanted to join us on the road,
to listen to our story, and to help us realize
that we are not walking in circles but moving
toward the house of peace and joy. This is the great mystery...
that continues to give us comfort and consolation:
we are not alone on our journey. The God of love who gave us life
sent us [His] only Son to be with us at all times and in all places,
so that we never have to feel lost in our struggles but always
can trust that God walks with us.

HENRI J. M. NOUWEN

Joy is the echo of God's life within us.

JOSEPH MARMION

Love comes while we rest against our Father's chest.
Joy comes when we catch the rhythms of His heart. Peace comes
when we live in harmony with those rhythms.

KEN GIRE

Joy is not happiness so much as gladness;
it is the ecstasy of eternity in a soul that has made peace with God
and is ready to do His will.

May the God of hope fill you with all
joy and peace as you trust in him.

ROMANS 15:13 NIV

Comfort Sweet

All God's glory and beauty come from within, and there He delights to dwell.
His visits there are frequent, His conversation sweet,
His comforts refreshing, His peace passing all understanding.

THOMAS À KEMPIS

God comforts. He doesn't pity. He picks us up, dries our tears,
soothes our fears, and lifts our thoughts beyond the hurt.

ROBERT SCHULLER

God comforts. He lays His right hand on the wounded soul…
and He says, as if that one were the only soul in all the universe:
O greatly beloved, fear not: peace be unto thee.

AMY CARMICHAEL

There is a place of comfort sweet
Near to the heart of God,
A place where we our Savior meet,
Near to the heart of God….
Hold us who wait before Thee
Near to the heart of God.

CLELAND B. MCAFEE

Every now and again take a good look at something not made with hands—
a mountain, a star, the turn of a stream. There will come to you
wisdom and patience and solace and, above all, the assurance
that you are not alone in the world.

SIDNEY LOVETT

*G*od is our merciful Father
and the source of all comfort.

2 CORINTHIANS 1:3 NLT

Drawn by Grace

Grace tells us that we are accepted just as we are.
We may not be the kind of people we want to be…
we may have more failures than achievements…
we may not even be happy,
but we are nonetheless accepted by God,
held in His hands.

McCullough

We throw open our doors to God and discover at the same moment
that he has already thrown open his door to us. We find ourselves
standing where we always hoped we might stand—
out in the wide open spaces of God's grace and glory.

Romans 5:2 msg

There is nothing but God's grace. We walk upon it; we breathe it;
we live and die by it; it makes the nails and axles of the universe.

Robert Louis Stevenson

The purpose of grace is primarily to restore our relationship with God….
The work of grace aims at…an ever deeper knowledge of God and an ever
closer fellowship with Him. Grace is God drawing us to Himself.

J. I. Packer

*W*e are made right with God by placing our faith in Jesus Christ.
And this is true for everyone who believes, no matter who we are.

ROMANS 3:22 NLT

Footpath to Peace

To be glad of life, because it gives you the chance to love
and to work and to play and to look up at the stars;
to be satisfied with your possessions, but not contented with yourself
until you have made the best of them…
to think seldom of your enemies, often of your friends,
and every day of Christ; and to spend as much time as you can,
with body and with spirit in God's out-of-doors—
these are little guideposts on the footpath to peace.

HENRY VAN DYKE

God's peace is joy resting. His joy is peace dancing.

F. F. BRUCE

You will go out in joy and be led forth in peace;
the mountains and hills will burst into song before you,
and all the trees of the field will clap their hands.

ISAIAH 55:12 NIV

Only God gives true peace—a quiet gift He sets within us
just when we think we've exhausted our search for it.

May the God of love and peace set your heart at rest
and speed you on your journey.

RAYMOND OF PENYAFORT

The LORD will give strength to His people;
the LORD will bless His people with peace.

Absolute Certainty

The hope we have in Christ is an absolute certainty.
We can be sure that the place Christ is preparing for us
will be ready when we arrive, because with Him nothing is left to chance.
Everything He promised He will deliver.

BILLY GRAHAM

Thank the Lord, it is His love that arranges our tomorrows—
and we may be certain that whatever tomorrow brings,
His love sent it our way.

CHARLES SWINDOLL

Faith is a living, daring confidence in God's grace,
so sure and certain that we could stake our life on it a thousand times.

MARTIN LUTHER

There is the firm commitment to the triumph
of the human spirit over adversity, the certainty
that there's a God on high who may not
move mountains but will give you the strength to climb.

GENEVA SMITHERMAN

Hope is definitely not the same thing as optimism.
It is not the conviction that something will turn out well,
but the certainty that something makes sense,
regardless of how it turns out.

VÁCLAV HAVEL

Now faith is being sure of what we hope for
and certain of what we do not see.

HEBREWS 11:1 NIV

Transforming Love

Love is patient and kind. Love is not jealous
or boastful or proud or rude. It does not demand its own way.
It is not irritable, and it keeps no record of being wronged.
It does not rejoice about injustice
but rejoices whenever the truth wins out.
Love never gives up, never loses faith, is always hopeful,
and endures through every circumstance....
Three things will last forever—faith, hope, and love—
and the greatest of these is love.

1 Corinthians 13:4–7, 13 NLT

Let your religion be less of a theory and more of a love affair.

G. K. Chesterton

God is love, and as much as I respond in allowing myself
to be transformed by that love and acting in that love,
that's my religion.

Bono

God is changeless. He will be unusual. He won't strike an average anywhere.
He will get out of bounds and meet us on any level with His patience
and His love and His bounty.

Jean Church

To love God, to serve Him because we love Him, is...
our highest happiness.... Love makes all labor light.
We serve with enthusiasm where we love with sincerity.

Hannah More

We trust as we love, and where we love. If we love Christ much,
surely we shall trust Him much.

THOMAS BENTON BROOKS

Enfolded in Peace

I will let God's peace infuse every part of today.
As the chaos swirls and life's demands pull at me on all sides,
I will breathe in God's peace that surpasses all understanding.
He has promised that He would set within me a peace too deeply planted
to be affected by unexpected or exhausting demands.

WENDY MOORE

Calm me, O Lord, as You stilled the storm,
Still me, O Lord, keep me from harm.
Let all the tumult within me cease,
Enfold me, Lord, in Your peace.

CELTIC TRADITIONAL

Nothing in all creation is so like God as stillness.

MEISTER ECKHART

Don't fret or worry. Instead of worrying, pray.
Let petitions and praises shape your worries into prayers,
letting God know your concerns. Before you know it,
a sense of God's wholeness, everything coming together for good,
will come and settle you down. It's wonderful what happens
when Christ displaces worry at the center of your life.

PHILIPPIANS 4:6–7 MSG

God cannot give us a happiness and peace apart from Himself,
because it is not there. There is no such thing.

C. S. LEWIS

....

....

....

....

....

....

....

....

....

....

....

....

....

....

....

....

....

....

*I am leaving you with a gift—
peace of mind and heart.*

JOHN 14:27 NLT

Radiant Grace

What do I love when I love You?
Not material beauty
or beauty of a temporal order;
not the brilliance of earthly light,
so welcome to our eyes;
not the sweet melody of harmony and song....
And yet, when I love Him,
it is true that I love a light
of a certain kind that I love in my inner self,
when my soul is bathed in light
that is not bound by space;
when it listens to sound that never dies away;
when it breathes fragrance that
is not borne away on the wind....
This is what I love when I love my God.

AUGUSTINE

Grace creates liberated laughter. The grace of God...
is beautiful, and it radiates joy.

KARL BARTH

Why did God give us imaginations? Because they help unfold His kingdom.
Imagination unveils the Great Imaginer. In the beginning, God created.
He imagined the world into being. Every flower, animal, mountain,
and rainbow is a product of God's creative imagination.

JILL M. RICHARDSON

He made you so you could share in His creation,
could love and laugh and know Him.

TED GRIFFEN

or the LORD God is our sun and our shield.
He gives us grace and glory.

PSALM 84:11 NLT

God So Loved

Who shall separate us from the love of Christ? Shall trouble or hardship
or persecution or famine or nakedness or danger or sword?...
No, in all these things we are more than conquerors
through him who loved us. For I am convinced
that neither death nor life, neither angels nor demons,
neither the present nor the future,
nor any powers, neither height nor depth,
nor anything else in all creation, will be able to separate us
from the love of God that is in Christ Jesus our Lord.

ROMANS 8:35, 37–39 NIV

All the things in this world are gifts and signs of God's love to us.
The whole world is a love letter from God.

PETER KREEFT

The grace of God means something like: Here is your life.
You might never have been, but you are because the party
wouldn't have been complete without you. Here is the world.
Beautiful and terrible things will happen. Don't be afraid. I am with you.
Nothing can ever separate us. It's for you I created the universe. I love you.

FREDERICK BUECHNER

Nothing can separate you from His love, absolutely nothing....
God is enough for time, and God is enough for eternity. God is enough!

HANNAH WHITALL SMITH

For God so loved the world
that he gave his one and only Son.

JOHN 3:16 NIV

The earth shall soon dissolve like snow,
The sun forbear to shine;
But God, who called me here below,
Will be forever mine.

JOHN NEWTON

Grace, because God is putting everything together again
through the Messiah, invites us into life—
a life that goes on and on and on, world without end.

ROMANS 5:21 MSG

God With Us

God gets down on His knees among us; gets on our level
and shares Himself with us. He does not reside afar off
and send diplomatic messages, He kneels among us....
God shares Himself generously and graciously.

EUGENE PETERSON

God is not really "out there" at all. That restless heart,
questioning who you are and why you were created,
that quiet voice that keeps calling your name
is not just out there, but dwells in you.

DAVID AND BARBARA SORENSEN

When all is said and done, the last word is Immanuel—
God-With-Us.

ISAIAH 8:10 MSG

God loves to look at us, and loves it when we will look back at Him.
Even when we try to run away from our troubles...God will find us, bless us,
even when we feel most alone, unsure.... God will find a way to let us know
that He is with us *in this place*, wherever we are.

KATHLEEN NORRIS

You are in the Beloved...therefore infinitely dear to the Father,
unspeakably precious to Him. You are never, not for one second, alone.

NORMAN DOWTY

*M*y Presence will go with you,
and I will give you rest.

EXODUS 33:14 NIV

Seeking Hearts

In extravagance of soul we seek His face. In generosity of heart,
we glean His gentle touch. In excessiveness of spirit, we love Him
and His love comes back to us a hundredfold.

TRICIA McCARY RHODES

I have been away and come back again many times to this place.
Each time I approach, I regret ever having left. There is a peace here,
a serenity, even before I enter. Just the idea of returning
becomes a balm for the wounds I've collected elsewhere.
Before I can finish even one knock,
the door opens wide and I am in His presence.

BARBARA FARMER

God's holy beauty comes near you, like a spiritual scent,
and it stirs your drowsing soul…. He creates in you the desire
to find Him and run after Him—to follow wherever He leads you,
and to press peacefully against His heart wherever He is.

JOHN OF THE CROSS

Once the seeking heart finds God in personal experience
there will be no problem about loving Him.
To know Him is to love Him
and to know Him better is to love Him more.

A. W. TOZER

You will seek me and find me
when you seek me with all your heart.

JEREMIAH 29:13 NIV

Hear My Prayer

Prayer can be a very intimate time with the Lord.
It is a one-on-one correspondence that allows you to express your heart,
your joys, and your praises to the One who will never fail or forsake you.

God wants His children to establish such a close relationship with Him that
He becomes a natural partner in all the experiences of life.

GLORIA GAITHER

We need quiet time to examine our lives openly and honestly....
Spending quiet time alone gives your mind an opportunity
to renew itself and create order.

SUSAN L. TAYLOR

God is our refuge and strength, always ready to help in times of trouble.

PSALM 46:1 NLT

Lord, hear my prayer. When I stumble over my words,
or when I can't find the right words to say, listen to my heart.
I want to talk with You. I want to walk with You. Hear me, O Lord,
and answer with grace and love and mercy. Take my hand
and my heart and lead me in prayer. Amen.

MARILYN JANSEN

The kiss of eternal life, and the warm embrace of God's Word,
are so sweet, and bring such pleasure, that you can never
become bored with them; you always want more.

HILDEGARD OF BINGEN

It is God's love for us that He not only
gives us His Word but also lends us His ear.

DIETRICH BONHOEFFER

Inner Sanctuary

Deep within us all there is an amazing inner sanctuary of the soul,
a holy place...to which we may continuously return. Eternity is at our hearts,
pressing upon our time-torn lives, warming us...calling us home unto Itself.
Yielding to these persuasions...utterly and completely, to the Light within,
is the beginning of true life.

THOMAS R. KELLY

Enter into the inner chamber of your mind.
Shut out all things save God and whatever may aid you in seeking God;
and having barred the door of your chamber, seek Him.

ANSELM OF CANTERBURY

Within each of us there is an inner place where the living God Himself
longs to dwell, our sacred center of belief.

The LORD your God is with you....
He will take great delight in you,
he will quiet you with his love,
he will rejoice over you with singing.

ZEPHANIAH 3:17 NIV

Have you ever thought what a wonderful privilege it is
that every one each day and each hour of the day has the liberty
of asking God to meet him in the inner chamber
and to hear what He has to say?

ANDREW MURRAY

The LORD is a shelter...a refuge in times of trouble.

PSALM 9:9 NLT

Immeasurable Love

We are so preciously loved by God that we cannot even comprehend it.
No created being can ever know how much and how sweetly
and tenderly God loves them. It is only with the help of His grace
that we are able to persevere in spiritual contemplation
with endless wonder at His high, surpassing, immeasurable love
which our Lord in His goodness has for us.

JULIAN OF NORWICH

God loved us, and through his grace he gave us a good hope
and encouragement that continues forever.

2 THESSALONIANS 2:17 NCV

The loving God we serve has immeasurable compassion
and tenderness toward each of us throughout our lives.

DR. JAMES DOBSON

The soul is a temple, and God is silently building it by night and by day.
Precious thoughts are building it; unselfish love is building it;
all-penetrating faith is building it.

HENRY WARD BEECHER

Our greatness rests solely on the fact that God in His
incomprehensible goodness has bestowed His love upon us.
God does not love us because we are so valuable;
we are valuable because God loves us.

HELMUT THIELICKE

$\mathcal{I}$n this is love, not that we loved God, but that He loved us.

1 JOHN 4:10 NASB

Open Hearts

The "air" which our souls need also envelops all of us at all times
and on all sides. God is round about us in Christ on every hand,
with many-sided and all-sufficient grace.
All we need to do is to open our hearts.

OLE HALLESBY

God wants you to know Him as personally as He knows you.
He craves a genuine relationship with you.... He didn't make us robots,
pre-programmed to love Him and follow Him. He gave us free will
and leaves it to us to choose to spend time with Him. That way it's genuine.
That way it's a real relationship.

TOM RICHARDS

What was invisible we behold,
What was unknown is known.
Open our eyes to the light of grace,
Unloose our hearts from fear,
Be with us in the strength of love,
Lead us in the hope of courage.

EVELYN FRANCIS CAPEL

Lord, give me an open heart to find You everywhere,
to glimpse the heaven enfolded in a bud,
and to experience eternity in the smallest act of love.

MOTHER TERESA

----

*God not only loves you very much but also has put
his hand on you for something special.*

1 THESSALONIANS 1:4 MS

New Every Morning

With God, life is eternal—both in quality and length.
There is no joy comparable to the joy of
discovering something new from God, about God.
If the continuing life is a life of joy,
we will go on discovering, learning.

EUGENIA PRICE

Take on an entirely new way of life—a God-fashioned life,
a life renewed from the inside and working itself into your conduct
as God accurately reproduces his character in you.

EPHESIANS 4:24 MSG

Each dawn holds a new hope for a new plan,
making the start of each day the start of a new life.

GINA BLAIR

In the morning let our hearts gaze upon God's love…
and in the beauty of that vision, let us go forth to meet the day.

ROY LESSIN

That is God's call to us—simply to be people who are content
to live close to Him and to renew the kind of life in which
the closeness is felt and experienced.

THOMAS MERTON

A quiet morning with a loving God puts the events
of the upcoming day into proper perspective.

JANETTE OKE

Satisfy us in the morning with your unfailing love,
that we may sing for joy and be glad all our days.

PSALM 90:14 NIV

Catch the Spirit

Grace binds you with far stronger cords than the cords
of duty or obligation can bind you. Grace is free,
but when once you take it, you are bound forever to the Giver
and bound to catch the spirit of the Giver. Like produces like.
Grace makes you gracious; the Giver makes you give.

E. STANLEY JONES

What makes life worthwhile is having a big enough objective,
something which catches our imagination
and lays hold of our allegiance…. What higher, more exalted,
and more compelling goal can there be than to know God?

J. I. PACKER

You called, You cried,
You shattered my deafness,
You sparkled, You blazed,
You drove away my blindness,
You shed Your fragrance,
and I drew in my breath,
and I pant for You.

AUGUSTINE

The grace of God…there's only one catch. Like any other gift,
the gift of grace can be yours only if you'll reach out and take it.
Maybe being able to reach out and take it is a gift too.

FREDERICK BUECHNER

As the deer pants for streams of water,
so my soul pants for you, O God.

PSALM 42:1 NIV

The Glory of the Son

The Son radiates God's own glory and expresses the very character of God,
and he sustains everything by the mighty power of his command.
When he had cleansed us from our sins, he sat down in the place of honor
at the right hand of the majestic God in heaven.

HEBREWS 1:3 NLT

In heaven our light will be provided by an infallible source, the Son of God.
And nothing will interfere with our basking in His fellowship.

MARILYN M. MORGAN

God also has highly exalted Him and given Him the name
which is above every name, that at the name of Jesus every knee should bow,
of those in heaven, and of those on earth,
and of those under the earth, and that every tongue
should confess that Jesus Christ is Lord,
to the glory of God the Father.

PHILIPPIANS 2:9–11 NKJV

The Word became human and made his home among us.
He was full of unfailing love and faithfulness. And we have seen his glory,
the glory of the Father's one and only Son.

JOHN 1:14 NLT

*T*urn your eyes upon Jesus, look full in His wonderful face,
and the things of earth will grow strangely dim,
in the light of His glory and grace.

HELEN H. LEMMEL

For Himself

The reason for loving God is God Himself, and the measure
in which we should love Him is to love Him without measure.

BERNARD OF CLAIRVAUX

Although it be good to think upon the kindness of God,
and to love Him and worship Him for it; yet it is far better
to gaze upon the pure essence of Him and to love Him
and worship Him for Himself.

We desire many things, and God offers us only one thing.
He *can* offer us only one thing—Himself. He has nothing else to give.
There *is* nothing else to give.

PETER KREEFT

You alone are the LORD. You made the heavens…,
the earth and all that is on it, the seas and all that is in them.
You give life to everything, and the multitudes of heaven worship you.

NEHEMIAH 9:6 NIV

There is an essential connection between experiencing God,
loving God, and trusting God. You will trust God only as much
as you love Him, and you will love Him to the extent you have touched Him,
rather that He has touched you.

BRENNAN MANNING

I live by faith in the Son of God,
who loved me and gave himself for me.

GALATIANS 2:20 NIV

Endless Grace

Grace is the dynamic outpouring of God's loving nature
that flows into and through creation in an endless
self-offering of healing, love, illumination, and reconciliation.
It is a gift that we are free to ignore, reject, ask for, or simply accept.

GERALD G. MAY

Because of his grace he declared us righteous
and gave us confidence that we will inherit eternal life.

TITUS 3:7 NLT

This GOD of Grace, this God of Love....
All that he makes and does is honest and true:
He paid the ransom for his people,
He ordered his Covenant kept forever.

PSALM 111:4, 7–9 MSG

We have been given the breath of life, designed with a unique,
one-of-a-kind soul that exists forever—whether we live it as a burden
or a joy or with indifference doesn't change the fact that we've
been given the gift of *being* now and forever.

WENDY MOORE

Let Jesus be in your heart,
Eternity in your spirit,
The world under your feet,
The will of God in your actions.
And let the love of God shine forth from you.

CATHERINE OF GENOA

*G*row in the grace and knowledge of our Lord and Savior Jesus Christ.
To him be glory both now and forever! Amen.

2 PETER 3:18 NIV

Forever Mine

We are always in the presence of God.... There is never
a non-sacred moment! His presence never diminishes.
Our awareness of His presence may falter,
but the reality of His presence never changes.

MAX LUCADO

The King of love my Shepherd is,
Whose goodness faileth never;
I nothing lack if I am His,
And He is mine forever.

SIR HENRY WILLIAMS BAKER

Whom have I in heaven but you?
And earth has nothing I desire besides you.
My flesh and my heart may fail,
but God is the strength of my heart
and my portion forever.

PSALM 73:25–26 NIV

God is always on duty in the temple of your heart, His home.... It is the place
where Someone takes your trouble and changes it into His treasure.

BARBARA JOHNSON

God is the sunshine that warms us, the rain that melts the frost
and waters the young plants. The presence of God is a climate
of strong and bracing love, always there.

JOAN ARNOLD

We have been in God's thought from all eternity, and in His creative love,
His attention never leaves us.

MICHAEL QUOIST

Surely goodness and love will follow me all the days of my life,
and I will dwell in the house of the LORD forever.

PSALM 23:6 NIV

When we've been there ten thousand years,
Bright shining as the sun,
We've no less days to sing God's praise
Than when we'd first begun.†

You have turned my mourning into joyful dancing…
that I might sing praises to you and not be silent.
O Lord my God, I will give you thanks forever!

Psalm 30:11–12 NLT

The Goal of Grace

This is the amazing story of God's grace.
God saves us by His grace and transforms us more and more
into the likeness of His Son by His grace. In all our trials and afflictions,
He sustains and strengthens us by His grace. He calls us by grace
to perform our own unique function within the Body of Christ.
Then, again by grace, He gives to each of us the spiritual gifts necessary
to fulfill our calling. As we serve Him, He makes that service acceptable
to Himself by grace, and then rewards us a hundredfold by grace.

JERRY BRIDGES

If God wants you to do something, He'll make it possible
for you to do it, but the grace He provides comes only with the task
and cannot be stockpiled beforehand. We are dependent on Him
from hour to hour, and the greater our awareness of this fact,
the less likely we are to faint or fail in a crisis.

LOUIS CASSELS

If you desire to be really happy, you must make
God your final and ultimate goal.

THOMAS À KEMPIS

It's not important who does the planting, or who does the watering. What's important is that God makes the seed grow.

1 CORINTHIANS 3:7 NLT

A New Day

God give me joy in the common things:
In the dawn that lures, the eve that sings.
In the new grass sparkling after rain,
In the late wind's wild and weird refrain;
In the springtime's spacious field of gold,
In the precious light by winter doled....
God give me joy in the tasks that press,
In the memories that burn and bless;
In the thought that life has love to spend,
In the faith that God's at journey's end.

THOMAS CURTIS CLARK

Every day we live is a priceless gift of God, loaded
with possibilities to learn something new, to gain fresh insights.

DALE EVANS ROGERS

You wake up in the morning, and lo! your purse is magically
filled with twenty-four hours of the magic tissue of the
universe of your life. No one can take it from you. No one receives
either more or less than you receive. Waste your infinitely precious
commodity as much as you will, and the supply will never be
withheld from you. Moreover, you cannot draw on the future.
Impossible to get into debt. You can only waste the passing moments.
You cannot waste tomorrow. It is kept for you.

ARNOLD BENNETT

The innocent brightness of a new born day is lovely yet.

WILLIAM WORDSWORTH

His compassions never fail. They are new every morning;
great is your faithfulness.

LAMENTATIONS 3:22–23 NIV

It Is Well

When peace like a river attendeth my way,
when sorrow like sea-billows roll;
Whatever my lot, Thou hast taught me to say,
"It is well, it is well with my soul."

HORATIO G. SPAFFORD

I have told you these things, so that in me you may have peace.
In this world you will have trouble. But take heart!
I have overcome the world.

JOHN 16:33 NIV

The peace of God is that eternal calm which lies far too deep down
to be reached by any external trouble or disturbance.

ARTHUR T. PIERSON

Only Christ Himself, who slept in the boat in the storm
and then spoke calm to the wind and waves,
can stand beside us when we are in a panic and say to us Peace.
It will not be explainable.
It transcends human understanding.
And there is nothing else like it in the whole wide world.

ELISABETH ELLIOT

How calmly may we commit ourselves
to the hands of Him who bears up the world.

JEAN PAUL RICHTER

The peace of God, which surpasses all understanding,
will guard your hearts and minds through Christ Jesus.

PHILIPPIANS 4:7 NKJV

Rich in Kindness

All praise to God, the Father of our Lord Jesus Christ,
who has blessed us with every spiritual blessing in the heavenly realms
because we are united with Christ. Even before he made the world,
God loved us and chose us in Christ to be holy and without fault in his eyes.
God decided in advance to adopt us into his own family
by bringing us to himself through Jesus Christ.
This is what he wanted to do, and it gave him great pleasure.
So we praise God for the glorious grace he has poured out on us who
belong to his dear Son. He is so rich in kindness and grace that he
purchased our freedom with the blood of his Son and forgave our sins.
He has showered his kindness on us,
along with all wisdom and understanding.

EPHESIANS 1:3–8 NLT

Herein is grace and graciousness! Herein is love and loving kindness!
How it opens to us the compassion of Jesus—so gentle, tender, considerate!

CHARLES H. SPURGEON

The LORD appeared to us...saying:
"I have loved you with an everlasting love;
I have drawn you with loving-kindness."

JEREMIAH 31:3 NIV

ᵍOD is all mercy and grace—
not quick to anger, is rich in love.

PSALM 145:8 MSG

Brand New Life

As the caterpillar finds its new ability to fly,
we should be thrilled over our Spirit-empowered ability
to live differently and faithfully. Isn't this what the Scriptures speak of?
Isn't this what we've all been longing for?

FRANCIS CHAN

This means that anyone who belongs to Christ
has become a new person. The old life is gone; a new life has begun!
All of this is a gift from God, who brought us back to himself through Christ.
And God has given us this task of reconciling people to him.
For God was in Christ, reconciling the world to himself,
no longer counting people's sins against them.
And he gave us this wonderful message of reconciliation.

2 CORINTHIANS 5:17–19 NLT

Jesus Christ is fully capable of bringing about change unto full restoration.
Just as His resurrection power brings new life, His redemption power brings
new hope. He is able, for He's more than a Savior! He's your Redeemer.

JACK HAYFORD

A life transformed by the power of God
is always a marvel and a miracle.

GERALDINE NICHOLAS

....

....

....

....

....

....

....

....

....

....

....

....

....

....

....

....

....

....

....

....

....

*Christ's one act of righteousness brings a right relationship
with God and new life for everyone.*

ROMANS 5:18 NLT

God of Grace

Look deep within yourself and recognize
what brings life and grace into your heart.
It is this that can be shared with those around you.
You are loved by God. This is an inspiration to love.

CHRISTOPHER DE VINCK

The Lord's chief desire is to reveal Himself to you and,
in order for Him to do that, He gives you abundant grace.
The Lord gives you the experience of enjoying His presence.
He touches you, and His touch is so delightful that,
more than ever, you are drawn inwardly to Him.

MADAME JEANNE GUYON

It is my calling to treat every human being with grace and dignity,
to treat every person, whether encountered in a palace or a gas station,
as a life made in the image of God.

SHEILA WALSH

To be grateful is to recognize the love of God
in everything He has given us—and He has given us everything.
Every breath we draw is a gift of His love, every moment of existence
is a gift of grace, for it brings with it immense graces from Him.

THOMAS MERTON

Set your hope fully on the grace to be given you
when Jesus Christ is revealed.

1 PETER 1:13 NIV

A Sense of Wonder

Whether sixty or sixteen, there is in every human being's heart
the love of wonder, the sweet amazement at the stars and starlike things,
the undaunted challenge of events, the unfailing childlike appetite
for what-next, and the joy of…living.

SAMUEL ULLMAN

Many, O LORD my God,
are the wonders which You have done,
And Your thoughts toward us;
There is none to compare with You
If I would declare and speak of them,
They would be too numerous to count.

PSALM 40:5 NASB

Dear Lord, grant me the grace of wonder.
Surprise me, amaze me, awe me in every crevice of Your universe….
Each day enrapture me with Your marvelous things without number.
I do not ask to see the reason for it all;
I ask only to share the wonder of it all.

ABRAHAM JOSHUA HESCHEL

Isn't it a wonderful morning?
The world looks like something God
had just imagined for His own pleasure.

LUCY MAUD MONTGOMERY

Loving Creator, help me reawaken my
childlike sense of wonder at the delights of Your world!

MARILYN MORGAN HELLEBERG

I will give thanks to the LORD with all my heart;
I will tell of all Your wonders.

PSALM 9:1 NASB

Love Interrupts

You know, what you put out comes back to you:
an eye for an eye, a tooth for a tooth, or in physics…
every action is met by an equal or an opposite one.…
And yet, along comes this idea called Grace to upend all that
"as you reap, so you will sow" stuff. Grace defies reason and logic.
Love interrupts, if you like, the consequences of your actions,
which…is very good news indeed.

BONO

Calvary is a telescope through which we look into the long vista of eternity
and see the love of God breaking forth into time.

MARTIN LUTHER KING JR.

I am amazed by the sayings of Christ. They seem truer than anything
I have ever read. And they certainly turn the world upside down.

KATHERINE BUTLER

When God has become our shepherd, our refuge, our fortress,
then we can reach out to Him in the midst of a broken world
and feel at home while still on the way.

HENRI J. M. NOUWEN

Grace is love that cares and stoops and rescues.

JOHN R. W. STOTT

_ive out your God-created identity. Live generously and graciously
toward others, the way God lives toward you.

MATTHEW 5:48 MSG

Life Light

You're here to be light, bringing out the God-colors in the world.
God is not a secret to be kept. We're going public with this,
as public as a city on a hill. If I make you light-bearers,
you don't think I'm going to hide you under a bucket, do you?
I'm putting you on a light stand. Now that I've put you there on a hilltop,
on a light stand—shine! Keep open house; be generous with your lives.
By opening up to others, you'll prompt people to open up with God,
this generous Father in heaven.

MATTHEW 5:14–16 MSG

In the beginning was the Word, and the Word was with God,
and the Word was God. He was with God in the beginning.
Through him all things were made;
without him nothing was made that has been made.
In him was life, and that life was the light of men.

JOHN 1:1–4 NIV

For you are all children of the light and of the day;
we don't belong to darkness and night.

1 THESSALONIANS 5:5 NLT

*W*e best glorify Him when His life
is seen through us as a light to others.

Connected by Grace

My vocation is grounded in belonging to Jesus,
and in the firm conviction that nothing
will separate me from the love of Christ.
The important thing is not how much we accomplish,
but how much love we put into our deeds every day.
That is the measure of our love for God.

MOTHER TERESA

God will never let you be shaken or moved from your place near His heart.

JONI EARECKSON TADA

I will remember that when I give Him my heart,
God chooses to live within me—body and soul.
He fills all of the empty places,
His very Spirit inside of me.

Dear God, whether all my prayers are short or long,
they are a way of keeping me connected to Your love.

LINDA NEUKRUG

Our God is so wonderfully good, and lovely,
and blessed in every way that the mere fact of belonging to Him
is enough for an untellable fullness of joy!

HANNAH WHITALL SMITH

Genuine love sees faces, not a mass:
the Good Shepherd "calls His own sheep by name."

GEORGE A. BUTTRICK

Fear not, for I have redeemed you;
I have called you by your name; You are Mine.

ISAIAH 43:1 NKJV

He Embraced Us

As for you, you were dead in your transgressions and sins....
But because of his great love for us, God, who is rich in mercy,
made us alive with Christ even when we were dead in transgressions—
it is by grace you have been saved. And God raised us up with Christ
and seated us with him in the heavenly realms in Christ Jesus,
in order that in the coming ages he might show
the incomparable riches of his grace,
expressed in his kindness to us in Christ Jesus.

EPHESIANS 2:4—7 NIV

There are times, and there will be times,
when it will be absolutely clear that only God's grace
keeps us from falling apart; and even if we cannot hold on to Him,
He will still hold on to us.

JOHANNES FACIUS

Those who live in the shelter of the Most High
will find rest in the shadow of the Almighty....
He will cover you with his feathers.
He will shelter you with his wings.
His faithful promises are your armor and protection.

PSALM 91:1, 4 NLT

....

....

....

....

....

....

....

....

....

....

....

....

....

....

....

....

....

....

....

....

Every whispered prayer sent heavenward
is our response to God's embrace.

JANET L. SMITH

The Wonder of Living

We need to recapture the power of imagination; we shall find
that life can be full of wonder, mystery, beauty, and joy.

SIR HAROLD SPENCER JONES

When I need a dose of wonder I wait for a clear night
and go look for the stars.... In the country the great river
of the Milky Way streams across the sky, and I know that our planet
is a small part of that river of stars.... Often the wonder
of the stars is enough to return me to God's loving grace.

MADELEINE L'ENGLE

May our lives be illumined
by the steady radiance
renewed daily,
of a wonder,
the source of which
is beyond reason.

DAG HAMMARSKJÖLD

Normal day, let me be aware of the treasure you are.
Let me learn from you, love you, bless you before you depart.
Let me not pass you by in quest
of some rare and perfect tomorrow.

The wonder of living is held within the beauty of silence,
the glory of sunlight...the sweetness of fresh spring air, the quiet strength
of earth, and the love that lies at the very root of all things.

The heavens praise your wonders, O LORD,
your faithfulness too, in the assembly of the holy ones.

PSALM 89:5 NIV

In His Kingdom

The needed change within us is God's work, not ours.
The demand is for an inside job, and only God can work from the inside.
We cannot attain or earn this righteousness of the kingdom of God:
it is a grace that is given.

RICHARD J. FOSTER

Then the way you live will always honor and please the Lord,
and your lives will produce every kind of good fruit.
All the while, you will grow as you learn to know God better and better....
For he has rescued us from the kingdom of darkness
and transferred us into the Kingdom of his dear Son,
who purchased our freedom and forgave our sins.

COLOSSIANS 1:10, 13–14 NLT

Nothing can compare to the beauty and greatness of the soul
in which our King dwells in His full majesty.
No earthly fire can compare with the light of its blazing love.
No bastions can compare with its ability to endure forever.

TERESA OF AVILA

High King of heaven, my victory won,
May I reach heaven's joys, O bright heaven's Sun!
Heart of my own heart, whatever befall,
Still be my Vision, O Ruler of all.

ELEANOR HULL

*Therefore, since we are receiving a kingdom which cannot be shaken,
let us have grace, by which we may serve God.*

HEBREWS 12:28 NKJV

I Believe

To believe in God starts with a conclusion about Him, develops into confidence in Him, and then matures into a conversation with Him.

Stuart Briscoe

I believe in God, the Father Almighty,
maker of heaven and earth.

And in Jesus Christ, His only Son, our Lord,
who was conceived by the Holy Spirit,
and born of the virgin Mary,
suffered under Pontius Pilate,
was crucified, dead, and buried.
He descended into hell.
The third day He rose again from the dead.
He ascended into heaven
and sitteth at the right hand of
God the Father Almighty.
From thence He will come to judge
the quick and the dead.

I believe in the Holy Spirit,
the Holy Christian Church,
the communion of saints,
the forgiveness of sins,
the resurrection of the body,
and the life everlasting. Amen.

The Apostles' Creed

The goal of grace is to create a love relationship between God
and us who believe, the kind of relationship for which
we were first made. And the bond of fellowship by which
God binds Himself to us is His covenant.

J. I. Packer

You have this faith and love because of your hope,
and what you hope for is kept safe for you in heaven.

COLOSSIANS 1:5 NCV

Bold I Approach

If heaven were by merit, it would never be heaven to me,
for if I were in it I should say, "I am sure I am here by mistake;
I am sure this is not my place; I have no claim to it."
But if it be of grace and not of works,
then we may walk into heaven with boldness.

CHARLES H. SPURGEON

You are a child of your heavenly Father. Confide in Him.
Your faith in His love and power can never be bold enough.

BASILEA SCHLINK

Love is there for us, love so great that it does not turn its face away from us.
That Love is Jesus. We can dare to hope and believe again.

GLORIA GAITHER

Whoso draws nigh to God
One step through doubtings dim,
God will advance a mile
In blazing light to him.

Never forget that through faith in Jesus, you have unlimited
and unhindered access to *the greatest father of all*, God.

DERWIN GRAY

Faith is the daring of the soul to go farther than it can see.

WILLIAM NEWTON CLARKE

Because of Christ and our faith in him, we can now come
boldly and confidently into God's presence.

EPHESIANS 3:12 NLT

Amazing Grace

ISBN 978-1-60936-035-1

Compiled by Barbara Farmer
Designed by Lisa & Jeff Franke

Printed in China.